ISBN 978-0-260-04751-9
PIBN 10924354

This book is a reproduction of an important historical work. Forgotten Books uses
state-of-the-art technology to digitally reconstruct the work, preserving the original format
whilst repairing imperfections present in the aged copy. In rare cases, an imperfection in
the original, such as a blemish or missing page, may be replicated in our edition. We do,
however, repair the vast majority of imperfections successfully; any imperfections that
remain are intentionally left to preserve the state of such historical works.

EXAMINATION

OF A

MINORITY REPORT

MADE BY THE

HON. ORVILLE CLARK,

TO THE

SENATE OF THE STATE OF NEW-YORK,

ON THE

MEMORIALS

OF INHABITANTS OF THE CITY OF NEW-YORK, IN RELATION TO

TRINITY CHURCH.

ALBANY:
PRINTED BY C. VAN BENTHUYSEN AND CO.
....
1846.

EXAMINATION

OF A

MINORITY REPORT

MADE BY THE

HON. ORVILLE CLARK,

TO THE

SENATE OF THE STATE OF NEW-YORK,

ON THE

MEMORIALS

OF INHABITANTS OF THE CITY OF NEW-YORK, IN RELATION TO

TRINITY CHURCH.

ALBANY:

PRINTED BY C. VAN BENTHUYSEN AND CO.

....

1846.

EXAMINATION

Of a minority report made by the Hon. Orville Clark, to the Senate of the State of New-York, on the memorials of inhabitants of the city of New-York, in relation to Trinity Church.

The committee on charitable and religious societies of the Senate of the State of New-York, to which were referred the memorials and remonstrances on the subject of legislative interference with the charter of Trinity church, having disagreed in their conclusions, two reports have been made by its members. One, by a majority of the committee recommending "that no legislative action be had on the subject, and that the prayer of the petitioners be denied;" the other by the Hon. Orville Clark, a senator from Washington county, recommending the repeal of the act of 1814. This report of Mr. Clark's occupies thirty-five pages, and contains so many extraordinary statements, and what are deemed erroneous representations of facts and documents, and so many inferences believed to be entirely unwarranted, as to require an exposition of its errors and fallacies by some one whose leisure will permit that thorough examination which it is hardly possible for a member of the Legislature to bestow, amid the numerous and various subjects which at this time occupy attention.

With the design, and in the hope of throwing some light on what Mr. Clark has rendered obscure, and of assisting an intelligent and impartial judgment, these pages have been prepared and are respectfully submitted for candid consideration. They will be confined to an examination of Mr. Clark's positions, and any repetition of the very able views of the majority of the committee will, as far as possible, be avoided. Nor will an attempt be made to notice many remarks and statements in Mr. Clark's report, which seem calculated rather to excite and inflame prejudice than to aid judgment, and which have a very remote, if any, bearing upon the questions at issue. This course is adopted to avoid excessive prolixity, with entire confidence in the intelligence of those for whose use these pages are intended, and in tneir determina-

4

tion to decide and act uprightly and conscientiously. In the style of these remarks, an effort will be made to imitate the modest and unassu-ming manner of the report of the majority of the committee, rather than the somewhat positive tone of Mr. Clark's report; and care will be taken not to affirm that to be undeniable, which admits of serious ques-tion, or to pronounce that impossible, which may have actually occurred.

Although the other members of the committee have differed from Mr. Clark so entirely in their conclusions, yet, a casual reader would infer from the language of his report, that the committee had really agreed on every important point, and concurred in the rseults. Thus in p. 7 it is said "*your committee* have no doubt or hesitation in stating the necessary effect of the treaty of peace of 1783," &c.; at p. 10, " But *your committee* are unable to admit the force or even the propriety of these observations." In p. 12, the language is quite inaccurate " your committee will state the grounds on which they recom-mend the entire repeal of ·the act of 1814." Surely *the committee* has made a very different recommendation. And the report at p. 35, thus closes: " your committee in conformity to the views they have express-ed, ask leave to introduce a bill." Without pursuing these references further, sufficient appears to show the carelessness with which the re-port has been ushered before the public, and to excite a doubt whether there may not be similar carelessness in other equally important portions of it.*

It is quite remarkable that Mr. Clark wholly repudiates the grounds on which the memorialists placed their case and solicited the interven-tion of the Legislature, and utterly denies the sufficiency of those grounds to justify the repeal of the act of 1814. He says "that the ques-tions which they involve are precisely those that the Legislature have no right to determine or [even] *consider*." (p. 33.) " If the memorial-ists really possess the right that they claim, they should be left to assert and vindicate them in a court of justice, since it is the exclusive pro-vince of a court of justice to establish the validity of their claims." (p. 33.) As this is the same conclusion expressed by the majority of the committee in their report, it would after all, seem that the committee were in fact unanimous. Still, Mr. Clark proceeds to say that " *the*

* It is due to the Hon. Senator to state, that the newspapers containing the account of the presentation of the minority report, added that Mr. Clark before reading it, apo-logised for its being in the form of a majority report, and engaged to alter it in that respect before delivering it to the printer. And the bill reported by him, purported to be brought in by Mr. Clark from the minority of the committee. Still, to readers who may never see the bill or the newspaper account, the report as printed is calcu-l ated to convey an entirely erroneous impression.

committee are of opinion that the access of the memorialists to a court of justice should no longer be barred, and that the impediment to the proper assertion of their rights, created by the act of 1814, should be removed."

The majority of the committee expressly deny that any obstacles exist to the legal assertion of the rights of the memorialists, because if the act of 1814 is unconstitutional, the courts will so declare. Mr. Clark has not stated with explicitness, or indeed at all, *how* the act of 1814 bars the access of the memorialists to a court of justice, or *how* it is an impediment to a proper assertion of their rights. This is a point which has been again and again presented to the memorialists and their advocates, and their attention invited to it. They have been asked, the Legislature has been asked, why interpose at all, when there is no occasion for it? And yet no answer is given—no necessity for the interposition is shown. The elaborate argument of Mr. Clark furnishes none, except that the act of 1814 is, in his opinion, a bad precedent of judicial legislation. He contends that it transcended the legitimate powers of the Legislature, that it violated rights secured by compact, but asserts that the memorialists should " be *left* to assert and vindicate them (those rights) in a court of justice;" and yet he would repeal an act which, if his argument proves any thing, is a perfect blank, is no bar, and presents no impediment whatever to the legal assertion of those rights. There are doubtless many bad precedents on the statute book, and some laws which our courts have pronounced unconstitutional. But, until the present instance, it is confidently believed no bill has been reported to expunge those precedents or to repeal those laws, merely because they were "mischievous in their effects," as examples, and therefore should be rendered "harmless by removal." Confidence in subsequent legislatures has been felt, that their own reason and intelligence would prevent their being led astray by unsound precedents or void laws. Mr. Clark does indeed say, (p. 27,) that "were it certain that courts of justice would give no effect to the act of 1814, the protection of the memorialists could not be said to require its repeal." But, he says *it is contended* that the act *is an absolute judgment of a court of competent jurisdiction and ultimate authority;* and then he says, the question arises whether *such an effect* can be given to the act without a violation of the principles of our constitution?" And he concludes that if this question must be answered in the negative, that is, if the act of 1814 be unconstitutional,—the only effectual mode of preventing an unjust application of it, is, to repeal it. With great deference this course seems to be quite a *non sequitur.* If the act be so clearly unconstitutional, there is no danger whatever of its being unjustly applied by the courts. And the very ground on which he thus recommends the repeal of the act, involves the necessity of this Legislature deciding that it was unconstitutional, and ought not therefore to be applied to the case for which it was intended; that is, for the Legislature to assume the functions of a court. How this is to be reconciled with the declaration at p. 33 of the same report, already quoted, that the Legislature has no right "to determine or consider" the question whether the act of 1814 was unconstitutional, must be left for others to determine. But the object of these remarks is not so much to exhibit what are supposed to be the contradictions of Mr. Clark's report, as to show that Mr. Clark himself cannot urge the repeal of the act of 1814 without calling upon the Legislature to act judicially.

This part of the subject ought not to be dismissed without a comment upon the extraordinary assertion above quoted from p. 27, that the remonstrants and their counsel contend that the effect to be attributed to the act of 1814, is that of an absolute judgment of a *court* of competent jurisdiction and ultimate authority. In no one of the published papers is any such principle contended for, and the gentlemen who attended before the committee absolutely deny that they ever advanced such an idea.* The argument was, and has been throughout, and is still, that it was competent to the Legislature, in its legislative capacity, *with the consent of the other party to the compact*, so to amend it, as to remove doubts, and prevent difficulties growing out of a change in the state of things. Any further exposition of this argument is postponed until we come to consider that subject distinctly, in a subsequent part of these remarks.

Dissatisfied, apparently, with the ground thus assumed, that the act was unconstitutional, and therefore should be repealed—a ground, as already stated which he repudiates in another part 'of his report, Mr. Clark proceeds to state in a formal manner, somewhat imposing, the grounds on which as he says *the committee*, but in fact himself only, recommends the repeal of the act of 1814. The first reason given at p. 12, 13, &c., is that the consent of the Legislature to the act of 1814, was induced by a misrepresentation of material facts; that the Legislature was misled—that both the fact and the law of the case

---

* It was urged by one of them who last addressed the committee, that whether the law of 1814 was or was not unconstitutional, was a question of law proper for the decision of the judicial department of the government; and he thought it strange that the Legislature should now be called upon to make this judicial decision by those who complained of the act of 1814, upon the ground that it was a judicial act which the Legislature ought not to have performed.

were misunderstood in consequence of the improper manner in which they were presented.

This is a very grave accusation, and ought to be sustained by proofs the most incontrovertible.

The misrepresentation—the deception, consists, according to Mr. Clark's report, in the applicants for the act of 1814, omitting to refer in terms and distinctly to the colonial act of 1704, as the charter, and the only subsisting charter of Trinity church; or as stated at p. 16, that the act of 1704 was "*virtually suppressed,*" that it was not referred to in the petition of Trinity church, nor in the pamphlets of Bishop Hobart or Col. Troup, except that it was mentioned in a note, in the latter; and that the Legislature were induced to suppose that it had been repealed, and that the charter of 1697 was operative until the act of 1784.

Each of those positions will be briefly examined in its order.

1st. As to the fact, what representations were made, and what evidence is there that the Legislature knew of the colonial act of 1704?

The petition of the corporation of Trinity church, embodied in their remonstrance to the present Legislature, and printed at p. 28 of a pamphlet containing the charter and other laws and proceedings relating to Trinity church, (and which will be herein referred to as *charter pamphlet,*) states the historical facts of its first incorporation, giving the date of 1697, and that it was the only parish church until some time after the revolution; it then recites the passage of the act of 1784, and quotes the provision it contains descriptive of the corporators. It then states that other Episcopal churches have been organized, and that some individuals belonging to such separate congregations have claimed a right to vote for wardens and vestrymen of Trinity church. It further represents that their corporate name has thus become inapplicable—it asks for an act altering the name, and to settle and obviate the questions that might arise in consequence of other Episcopal congregations in New-York being incorporated. The petition is brief, but explicit, and fairly and truly presents the evils for which a remedy was sought. It will be seen that there was a distinct and unequivocal reference to the act of 1784.

The law passed upon this petition in 1814 contains a preamble reciting the act of 1784 by its title in full; and also reciting the act of 10th March, 1788, enabling the corporation to take a different name, and which name, it recites they pray may be altered: and it makes alterations in both those acts.

Here then is indubitable evidence that the acts of 1784 and 1788 were before, and known to, the Legislature which passed the law of 1814.

Now the act of 1788 has a preamble, *reciting the colonial act of 27th June* 1704, and stating that it was repealed in 1784, but that the corporation had continued to use the name therein specified, and thereupon it enacts that the corporation may take and use a new name.

And the preamble to the act of 1784 recites the charter of 1697, *it recites and gives in full the title of the colonial act of* 1704, it declares that provisions in both the charter and the colonial act were inconsistent with the spirit and letter of the constitution of this state, and the act amends and alters both of them. Again, the preamble to the sixth section *recites in full the title of the colonial act of* 1704, with the date of its passage, and in the body of the same section *again repeats the title of that act*, and repeals it absolutely.

After this how can it be said that the colonial act of 1704 was unknown to the Legislature of 1814, that it was virtually suppressed? It was impossible for any member of the Legislature to vote upon the bill understandingly without recurring to the acts of 1784 and 1788, which it professed to amend and alter. And he could not look at those acts without seeing that the colonial act of 1704 was five times recited or distinctly referred to. If this be a mode of *suppressing* a fact, it would be desirable to know by what means it shall be made known.

But, says Mr. Clark, the Legislature was misled by having their attention drawn to the charter of 1697 by the pamphlets of Bishop Hobart and Col. Troup, and by the omission of those pamphlets to refer to the colonial act of 1704. It must have escaped Mr. C's observation that the pamphlet of Col. Troup was never before the Legislature at all, previous to the passage of the bill through the two houses. It was written and published *after* Chancellor Lansing had reported his objections to the bill, to the council of revision—for it contains those objections at large, and its object was to answer and remove them. If, therefore, it misled the Legislature in the passage of the bill, it must have been by some singular *ex post facto* operation of which there is probably no other instance on record.

As to the pamphlet attributed to Bishop Hobart, an examination of it will show that he discusses the question solely and exclusively as it arose upon the 3d section of the act of 1784, and upon the act of 1788. There is not one single idea or remark founded upon the charter of 1697, and indeed that charter is not mentioned, nor is there any allusion to it, except that in the commencement of the pamphlet, the *fact* is stated that "since the year of our Lord 1697 a corporation in the city of New-York styled the corporation of Trinity church, have enjoyed a charter," &c. The idea of its being possible for Bishop Hobart to make an attempt to mislead the Legislature, would require the strongest proof to satisfy any one acquainted with the character of that estimable man; and when an inspection of his pamphlet shows how utterly destitute of foundation such an idea is, his friends and the friends of truth, justice and fair dealing, will lament that it should have been so inconsiderately avowed.

Before dismissing this point let us enquire how far the principle itself is tenable, that a law should be repealed, because the applicants for it took a wrong view of their case, presented facts and arguments conformable to that view, made no *mistatement* of any fact, perverted none, but omitted to bring into view a law on the public statute book, which they honestly supposed to be repealed, and which law must necessarily come under the examination of any one seeking to inform himself on the subject? Stripped of all exaggeration and amplification, this is really the sum and substance of Mr. Clark's complaint, assuming the correctness of all his representations on the subject. And the mere statement of the case, would seem to be sufficient, without further answer.

The analogy which Mr. Clark institutes at p. 23 between acts of the Legislature and private contracts being avoided by misrepresentation or concealment of material facts, is unfortunate for his position. As to misrepresentation of any *fact*, it is out of the question; it is not pretended that there was any; the only allegation is that there was a concealment of a law. Chancellor Kent in his 39th lecture, thus states the principle: "If there be an intentional concealment or suppression of material facts in the making of a contract, in cases in which *both parties* have not equal access to the means of information, it will be deemed unfair dealing and will vitiate and avoid the contract." "As a general rule, each party is bound to communicate to the other his knowledge of material facts, *provided* he knows the other to be ignorant of them, and they be not open and marked, or equally within the reach of his observation." Even this rule, the learned chancellor in a note admits to be too broad, and should be qualified so as to require that the party in possession of facts, must be *under some special obligation*, by confidence reposed, or otherwise, to communicate them truly and fairly. But take the rule in its broadest sense, and it will be seen how decisive it is against the position of Mr. Clark. For no one will pretend that the Legislature "had not equal access to the means of information," with the applicants, or that a printed and published statute "was not equally within the reach" of the Legislature as it was of every citizen.

There are some collateral matters under this head, which it may be well to notice, although they have a slight bearing, if any, upon the point.

At p. 14, it is remarked, that "it is evident from the report made by the Attorney-General to the Assembly, that his opinion ws founded solely on the charter of 1697 and on the acts of 1784 and 1788." The language of the Attorney-General is this: "that he has examined a printed copy of the charter granted in 1697 to the Rector, &c., *and the acts altering the said charter*, together with the bill, &c., and that he is of opinion that the passage of the said bill will not defeat or vary any existing vested rights under the said charter and *acts*." The plain inference from this language, strengthened by the reflection that no honest attorney-general would give an opinion upon any subject, without examining *all* the laws bearing on it, is that Mr. VAN VECHTEN looked into the colonial act of 1704, as well as the acts of 1784 and 1788.

It must excite some surprise to witness these labored efforts to show that the highly respectable applicants for the law of 1814 made a misre-presentation, by a very foolish and necessarily futile attempt to conceal a public law,—that the Attorney-General neglected the duty of investigat-ing the matter referred to him, by omitting to look for or consider a law having connection with that matter, and to stultify the whole Legislature by the supposition that they were not only ignorant of a law now said to be so material, but that they were hoodwinked and prevented from look-ing at it, by the omission of the petitioners to quote it and spread it be-fore them.

2. If the applicants presented their case to the Legislature of 1813, under the belief that the colonial act of 1704 was not in existence,—that it had been repealed and had no influence upon the existing rights of the corporation, and if the Legislature acted under the same impres-sion,—they were correct in law and in fact; and the representation was true, and the arguments, if any, founded upon it, were just and sound; in other words, assuming all that is alleged by Mr. Clark, to have been represented to the Legislature, there was no misrepresentation—no deception. Aware that the settlement of this question of fact must dis-pose of the first reason given by him for the repeal of the act of 1814, Mr. Clark labors with great ingenuity to establish the position that the colonial act of 1704 was not wholly repealed by the act of 1784. Let us take his own statement of the law: "The 6th section of that law" (of 1784,) he says, at p. 84, " *enumerates* the colonial act of 1704 in the list of those

that it *expressly repeals*, and this repeal, looking merely at the words there used, is *absolute* and *total.*" One would suppose that after such an admission, the question would be at rest. But the report under consideration is remarkable for the alacrity with which the most obstinate facts and the clearest provisions of law, are combatted and wrestled with. In this instance, it is said that this absolute and total repeal is to be restrained by what is assumed to be the manifest intention of the Legislature to repeal only such parts as were inconsistent with the provisions of the constitution ; and as *some* of the provisions of the act of 1704 were not of that character, a court of law would hold that they were not included in that repeal. If courts of law adhere to what they have already said, they will hold a very different language. The fundamental maxim quoted by Chancellor Kent in his 20th lecture, seems peculiarly adapted to this case : *Quoties in verbis nulla est ambiguitas, ibi nulla expositio contra verba expressa, fienda est. Co. Litt.* 147. *Wing.* 24; thus translated in Branch's Principia: *When in the words there is no ambiguity, no exposition contrary to the words is to be made.* The judges said in *Edrick's* case, (5 *Rep.* 118, *b*,) "that they ought not to make any construction against the express letter of the statute ; for nothing can so express the meaning of the makers of the act, as their own direct words." In 1 *Term Rep.* 51, Justice Ashurst says, " it is safer to adopt what the Legislature have actually said, than to suppose what they meant to say." These authorities might be multiplied almost indefinitely to show that interpretation according to a supposed intent, is not to be indulged against the plain words of a statute, and that it is only when the words are in themselves ambiguous, or where they would produce manifest injustice, or be absurd, that it is allowable to examine the intent.

A further reason given by Mr. Clark for denying that the colonial act of 1704 was repealed by the act of 1784, is that the latter act would thereby be rendered contradictory in its various provisions. The first section, after repealing certain parts of the charter of 1697, and of the colonial act of 1704, declares that " nothing in this law shall be in any wise construed to annul, injure, repeal or make void the said charter or the said law, where the same are not inconsistent with the constitution of this State." And yet, it is admitted by Mr. Clark that in a subsequent section, the 6th, the colonial act of 1704 is repealed by words that are " absolute and total," and that the repeal is " entire and absolute in its terms."* To prevent this manifest contradiction, which however

---

* If it were at all necessary to account for this contradiction in the act of 1784, it might be done by reference to the Assembly Journals of that year, p. 47, where it appears that the bill was amended in committee of the whole of that house ; and by re.

is beyond the power of human ingenuity, he would restrict the "absolute terms," and make that a "*partial*" repeal which he admits to be *entire*. But a contradiction in a statute is a much less evil, than a defiance of the expressed, explicit and undenied will of the Legislature; and the rule in such cases has been settled for centuries, and adhered to without ever being questioned by any judicial decision. That rule was given in the case of the *Attorney-General* vs. *The Governor and Company of Chelsea Water-works*, reported in Fitzgibbon, p. 195; it is that a proviso directly repugnant to the body or provision of the act, shall stand, and be held to be a repeal of the preceding enactment, by analogy to the well known rule of construction applicable to testamentary instruments— that a later clause, if inconsistent with a former one, expresses the last intention, and revokes the preceding expressions. The rule as quoted from Fitzgibbon is given in Bacon's Abridgement, title *Statute*, and in 2 Dwarris Stat. 675, as the undoubted law. In the case of *the King* vs. the *Justices* of *Middlesex*, 2 Barn. and Ad. 818, Chief Justice, Lord Tenterden quoted and referred to the same decision in Fitzgibbon as the existing law, and he applied the principle that the latest enactment *speaks the last intention* of the makers, to the case before the court, where two contradictory acts were passed in the same session of parliament, to come into operation on the same day; and the court accordingly held that "the act which last received the royal assent must have the effect of repealing the other."

The same principle was again recognized and applied by the English court of common pleas, as late as 1835, in the case of Paget, and another *vs.* Foley, reported in 2 Bingham's New Cases, p. 679. Hence it will be seen that courts do not regard contradictions in the same statute, or between different statutes, as any reason for disregarding the plain words of an act. They have regarded consistency in acts as much less important than the *certainty* arising from a firm and well settled rule.

---

ference to p. 117, where it appears that the bill had also received amendments in the Senate. We have no direct evidence of the nature of those amendments, but there are strong reasons which would occupy too much space here, for believing that the 6th section was added in the Senate, without adverting to the incongruity of a total repeal of an act which in a previous section had been repealed in part.

It is worthy of note that *three* of the acts repealed by the 6th section of the act so often quoted, chap. 33, which was passed 17th April, 1784, were also repealed by their titles in full, by the act chap. 38, which was passed on the 20th of April 1784, and that another act, *a part* of which was repealed by the above chap. 33 was wholly repealed by chap. 38. These acts were pending at the same time, as appears by the Journal. Thus showing that it was not deemed extraordinary to repeal wholly an act that was already partially repealed, or to repeat the repeal of other acts.

It is not deemed necessary to add any thing to this authorative rule. It speaks for itself, and shows, it is believed, beyond the reach of dispute, that the colonial act of 1704 was repealed absolutely, by the act of 1784, notwithstanding the declaration in a previous part of the same statute. Still, it may be proper to refer to the act of 1788, which recites explicity that the colonial act of 1704 was repealed by the law of 1784. As the almost contemporary opinion of a whole Legislature, it is entitled to at least as much respect as that of a single Senator, given sixty years afterwards.

Of course if any representation was made to the Legislature of 1813, that the colonial act of 1704 was repealed—such representation was true, and any inferences which were drawn from the fact were fully justified.

And thus, it would seem certain that the first reason assigned by Mr Clark for the repeal of the act of 1814, that it was procured under a misrepresentation, or a " suppression " of the colonial act of 1704, falls to the ground.

Mr. Clark contends (p. 7 and 8) that the charter of Trinity church, whether it consisted of the letters patent issued in 1697, or of the colonial act of 1704, became extinct by the revolution, and that the act of 1784 was necessary "to reanimate a lifeless corporation." The point has so little practical bearing on the questions at issue, as scarcely to justify an extended discussion, and yet the position is deemed so unsound that it ought not to pass without comment. The Supreme Court of this State and that of the United States, have by a series of decisions established beyond all controversy, that the division of an empire does not in any manner impair or affect private or corporate rights; that our revolution left the corporations created under British authority in full vigor and possessed of all the franchises which could be enjoyed consistently with our forms of government. *Terret* vs. *Tayler*, 9 Cranch 43, 50, was a decision to that effect, relating particularly to Episcopal churches in Virginia; and *the Society for propagating the gospel* vs. *New Haven*, in 8 Wheaton 481, as well as *Dartmouth College* vs. *Woodward*, 4 Wheaton, 706, were repetitions of the same doctrine applied to other corporations. See also 1 *John. Cases*, 29, 32; 3d *do.* 109. The idea broached by Mr. Clark, that it was a *condition* of the charter of Trinity Church that the corporators should remain in the communion of the church of England as established and *governed* by the laws of England, is believed to be a mere assumption without any foundation other than a vivid fancy. It might be said with far greater plausibility, that the *political* charters of the cities of New-York and Albany, were subject to the condition of being under the goveroment of Great Britain.

Trinity Church was a religious corporation; the religious denomination of its corporators was *described*, not prescribed, as being in communion of the church of England as by law established. This was a communion of faith, doctrine and worship, exclusively religious, and without any necessary connexion with the civil government. In the preface to the Book of Common Prayer of the American Episcopal church, after speaking of the alterations that had been made, which it says will appear, upon a comparison with the book of Common Prayer of the church of England, proceeds thus: "In which it will also appear that this church is far from intending to depart from the church of England in any essential point of doctrine, discipline or worship; or further than local circumstances require." This communion may and does exist between citizens and subjects of different countries, without the least reference to their respective civil governments; as in the case of the Friends or Quakers in England and America ; Presbyterians in Scotland and in our country ; Methodists m the two countries, &c., &c.—and it may exist even when the respective nations are at war. The connexion of the Episcopal church in England with the civil government was a mere incident, in no way necessary to the religious character or communion of the church, as is evident from the fact that in Scotland the Episcopal is not the established church, and yet its members are in communion with the church of England, and the latter are in communion with the Scottish church. The same relations exist between the Episcopal church in America and that in England; our ministers preach in their churches; theirs officiate in ours ; the members of both reciprocally partake of the communion in the churches of both nations—and there never has been an interruption of that communion with the church of England, by the corporators of Trinity church from 1697 to this day. The object of Mr. Clark in the remarks which have just been quoted, was to exhibit the necessity of the act of 1784, "to reanimate, as he terms it, a lifeless corporation." The propriety of such an act and the necessity of some of its provisions are admitted, and it was certainly desirable, considering the circumstances in which the corporation had been placed by the war of the revolution and the occupation of the city by British troops, that the now independent State should, by a legislative act, remove all doubts, settle conflicting claims, and enable Trinity Church to execute its high mission. The act of 1784 was passed for this purpose. It does not contain any terms of incorporation, but it attains the object of reviving that which had been in abeyance, and of imparting to it new vigor, by appointing of its own authority a set of wardens and vestrymen, (sect. 4,) by declaring who should thereafter be corporators, (sect.

3,) and by confirming its original charter after amending and modifying it to the altered circumstances. (Sec. 1 and 2.) This revival, recognition and establishment of the charter of 1697 was effected by the first section of the act, which, after reciting that charter and the colonial act of 1704, provides that "nothing in this law, and no non-user or mis-user, &c. shall be construed to annul, injure, repeal, or make void *the said charter*, or the said law, &c. where the same are not inconsistent with the constitution of this State." Can language be more explicit in recognising the existence of the charter, and the validity of all its provisions, *excepting* those inconsistent with the constitution of this State ?

How needless was the exception if the other provisions were invalid ? Is this not precisely the case in which the sound and venerated maxim of the common law and of common sense applies with irresistible force ? *Exceptio probat regulam de rebus non exceptis;* 11 Co., 41. An exception proves the rule in things not excepted.

If then, the position of Mr. Clark at p. 5, be correct that it was *indispensable* to enable Trinity Church to continue a living and active corporation, that an act of the Legislature should be passed designating the corporators, and *defining the mode of their action ;* and that this was the object of the act of 1784, it will be seen at once by an inspection of that act that it wholly fails in this object unless it be coupled with the charter of 1697, or the colonial law of 1704 ; for the act itself contains nothing *defining the mode of action of the corporators ;* it confers no corporate powers in direct terms; it does not even fix the number of vestrymen, nor the time of their election, nor does it prescribe any of their duties or powers. But it couples itself with the charter of 1697, as already explained, corrects its defects and engrafts its own provisions upon it, and thus sets the machinery in motion. It is submitted that this is a fair, just and reasonable view of that act, and the only one which renders it what Mr. Clark says it should have been and was intended to be.

In a note to his report at p. 19, Mr. Clark says "if the charter of 1697 were superseded or abrogated by the subsequent act of the Assembly, (the colonial law of 1704,) express words were palpably necessary to create or restore its validity. The mere repeal of the colonial act would not have that effect." It is utterly denied that the colonial law of 1704 either suspended or abrogated the charter of 1697. On the contrary it is maintained that it did not create anew any corporation. It contains no expressions of that character usual in acts of incorporation; but in the very first section, recognized one as then existing, by enacting that " the rector and inhabitants of the said city of New-York in communion of the church of England, as by law established, and their successors, shall be capable of suing, &c., by the name of *the rector and inhabitants of the city of New-York, in communion of the Church of England, as by law established.*" It thus describes a rector as already existing, which could not be without a lawful church, of which there could be a rector. In truth it describes the corporation created by the charter of 1697, which, it is therein declared, shall be a body corporate, by the name of " the rector and inhabitants of our said city of New-York, in communion of our Protestant Church of England, as now established by our laws." It is obvious that these were not intended as the very words of the name, as the phrases "*our* city of New-York," "*our* protestant church," and "estab-lished by *our* laws," could not be used with propriety in any instrument executed by the corporation, or in any contract with it by any other party than the crown, or in any act by a third party. In such cases, the word " our" must necessarily be omitted, and the word " the" substituted. With that change, which was obviously proper in an act of the colonial legislature, it will be seen that the name recited in the commencement of the first section of the colonial act of 1704, is identical with that by which the corporation is described in the charter, with the exception of the word " protestant," which was a pleonasm, as the church of England was notoriously protestant. It is supposed that if the same name had been used in a grant of property to the corporation, or in a contract with it, no one would have doubted that it was well and sufficiently described. "The name of a corporation frequently consists of several words, and the transposition, interpolation, omission or alteration of some of them, may make no es-sential difference in their sense." 1 *Kyd*, 227. In Angel and Ames on Corporations, p. 55, a variety of cases are collected, showing the settled law that any such omissions or alterations are regarded as immaterial. If to these considerations be added the established rule that the law does not favor repeals by implication, and that two statutes are to stand together if possible, (9 *Cowen*, 437,) it will be a very fair conclusion that the colonial act of 1704 did not supersede or abrogate the charter of 1697 any further than as their provisions were inconsistent, which was the case in a very few and not important particulars.

But Mr. Clark, assuming that the charter was already abrogated by the colonial act of 1704, says that " express words were palpably necessary to create or restore its validity. The mere repeal of the colonial act would not have that effect." To this it is replied that there is no doctrine bet-ter settled by a uniform current of decisions, and by the acknowledgment of all the elementary writers than this, which is thus given in the words of Blackstone: "If a statute that repeals another is itself repealed afterwards, the first statute is hereby revived without any formal words for that purpose." 1 *Comm.* 90. If the rule had been drawn up expressly to negative Mr. Clark's position, it could not have been more direct. In 7 *Cowen*, 536, 537, the rule is recognized and applied; and probably hundreds of cases might be cited where it has been adopted and enforced.

It may be expected in this connexion, that some remarks should be made upon the observations of Mr. Clark, at p. 5, 6, &c., intended to show that the colonial act of 1704 was regarded by the government and the corporation itself as the only law which governed the corporation previous to the act of 1784. So far as any practical results could follow from the admission, it might with perfect safety be admitted. For it has been shown, it is hoped satisfactorily, that the colonial act was repealed in 1784, and if the charter of 1697 had been overshadowed by or merged in it, it was revived and restored in full force by the same act of 1784. It therefore becomes quite immaterial to enquire how it was regarded during the time it was in operation. But the statements of Mr. Clark upon this point are deemed so erroneous, that a brief space may properly be devoted to their correction. It is said at p. 6, that the grant made in 1705 is made to the exact corporate name that the act of 1704 imposed, and that the preamble of the grant refers to this act as the *sole* origin of the corporate power of the corporation. This is believed to be an exaggeration of the language of the preamble. It was natural that the reference should be to the more recent charter, which had passed but a year previous, conferring full powers to take and hold real estate; which reference was sufficient for all the purposes of the recital, and it would have been mere surplussage to refer to the charter of 1697. Surely it is a strained inference to draw from the mere naming of one out of two, or out of a dozen, acts of incorporation, that the others were obsolete or extinct; and as to the name of the corporation, it has already been shown that it was sufficiently identical in the two instruments, to prevent any ambiguity.

It is said in the same page that the right of voting for wardens and vestrymen of Trinity Church was limited in its actual exercise to the *communicants* of the church. And then it is averred that this limitation is to be found *only* in the act of 1704. Now it is asserted with great confidence that the limitation of the electoral right, so far as it required the voters to be communicants was the same in the charter of 1697, and in the colonial act of 1704; and that at all events there was great reason for such a construction—which would of itself account for the practice, and be sufficient to preclude the inference attempted to be drawn from the fact.

3

In the charter of 1697, (p. 9, Charter Pamphlet,) the qualifications of voters is thus described, "by the majority of the inhabitants of the said parish *in communion as aforesaid*"—the communion thus referred to, is described in an antecedent part of the same clause as that of " our protestant church of England." Mr. Clark says, at p. 6, that "according to the well known doctrines of that church, its communion embraces all its members; in other words all belong to the communion of the church who have been baptized or confirmed therein, and have not explicitly renounced its doctrines." This statement is far from being correct. By the doctrines of that church, all who have been baptised in it are members of the church; but it is not essential to membership that they should be communicants. Members, not communicants, are not described in any of its offices or by its accredited writers, as being *in communion* with it. The term " communion " in a religious sense, is peculiar to the episcopal church, and is not used in the same sense in the written religious devotions or services of any other denomination. Its prayer book denominates as the " holy communion " that sacrament which other churches call " the Lord's supper."

This word " communion " may be used in various senses: that which is intended by its use in the charter and in the colonial act, is the one very accurately given by Dr. Webster, " the act of communicating the sacrament of the eucharist; the celebration of the Lord's supper." This will appear from an examination of different parts of the colonial act of 1704. The 3d section of that act, (p. 18, Charter Pamphlet,) provides that the right of presentation to the rectorship, shall belong " to the church wardens and vestrymen of the said church, annually elected or to be elected by the inhabitants aforesaid, *in communion as aforesaid*." The 5th section declares that the rector and inhabitants *in communion* as aforesaid, may have a common seal. The 6th section enacts " that it shall and may be lawful for the *inhabitants aforesaid*, (as yet described only as being *in communion*) to assemble and meet together, &c., and choose wardens and vestrymen, communicants of the said church, by the majority of the voice of *the said communicants so met*, and not otherwise." Here the word " communicants " is for the first time introduced, and is applied to *inhabitants in communion* assembled and met together. A subsequent part of the same 6th section provides as follows: " and in case the church wardens or vestrymen, or any of them, happen to die within the year, it shall be lawful for the inhabitants aforesaid *in communion* as aforesaid, at any time upon such emergency to meet at the said church, upon notice given by the rector to elect and choose others so qualified as aforesaid, in their room," &c. It will scarcely be contended by any one, that the act intended to prescribe a particular qualification for electors in the choice of vestrymen at the *annual* election, and a different one for the choice of the same officers at a *special election* to supply vacancies. A view of all these sections would induce a very satisfactory conclusion that the same description of persons were intended, whether described as "communicants" or as being "in communion" with the church of England. The same expression in the charter of 1697, being "in communion" doubtless referred to the same description of persons. The view which Col. Troup takes of this question in his pamphlet, p. 31, 32, is evidence at least of the construction of intelligent men of that day. "The language of the charter and law, (colonial law of 1704,) is no less intelligible than its meaning is clear, and the mind that could doubt whether communicants alone are entitled to vote, must have been incurably diseased with skepticism."

Mr. Clark has himself furnished the means of presenting a very satisfactory argument why the Legislature should not interpose to repeal the act of 1814, even if it were founded upon misrepresentation and suppression of fact. He refers, at p. 23, 24, to the provisions of the Revised Statutes, authorizing a *scire facias* to be issued against any corporation for the purpose of vacating and annulling any act creating, &c., such corporation, " on the ground that the same was passed upon some fraudulent suggestion or concealment made by the persons incorporated by such act, or made with their consent or knowledge." (*2d Rev. Stat., p.* 479, § 13, *2d edition.*) This section is doubtless, merely in affirmance of the common law, by which a *scire facias* may issue out of Chancery to repeal any patent. *Comyn's Dig. Patent, F,* 6. At all events the power of the Court of Chancery over the subject cannot be denied. *5 Cruise's Dig.,* 53, 55. In one of the modes stated, either by *scire facias* or by bill in chancery, the question of misrepresentation, of suppression of facts, can be tried if the Legislature desire it, and the consequences be visited upon those by whose instrumentality it was produced.

If then, the memorialists are convinced by Mr. Clark's remarks, of the evidence of such an extraordinary fact, that the Legislature of 1813 were by some species of mesmerism, or other unaccountable influence, kept in profound ignorance of a law on the printed statute book, referred to in the act which they were amending—a fact which, it is presumed, the memorialists had not themselves discovered when they prepared and presented their petitions for the repeal of the act of 1814, (for those petitions contain no allusion whatever to it;) if they are satisfied of this fact, and believe that it ought to vitiate the legislation which was predicated on such profound ignorance and consummate folly, let them ask the Legislature to authorize legal proceedings to ascertain it. It is be-lieved that they will meet with no opposition from the corporation of Trinity Church or their friends.

II. The second reason given by Mr. Clark for a repeal of the act of 1814, (p. 12, 24, &c.,) is that it was the exercise of *a judicial* power, un-warranted and dangerous. He says, " it is *admitted* that if it altered the existing rights of the corporators, it was a plain violation of the Con-stitution of the United States," for which he refers in a *note* to the pre-face to the re-print of remarks on Trinity Church bill, by Col. Troup. Now that preface has been examined again and again, with the utmost care, and no such admission, nor any approaching it, can be found. Judge Troup had contended in his pamphlet that it was competent to the Legislature to alter the elective franchise in corporations without advert-ing to the distinction between public corporations, employed in the ad-ministration of the government, and private eleemosynary institutions. It was to correct this omission that the preface in question called attention to this distinction, as established in cases decided since the appearance of the pamphlet, and as prohibiting the intervention of the Legislature in relation to private corporations *without their consent.* The only question discussed was the right of the Legislature to interfere *against the will of the corporation,* for that is the only case to which the constitutional pro-hibition applies. If the contract be modified by the consent of the con-tracting parties, the obligation is not impaired—the obligation no longer remains, it has been removed by the parties. This is a principle which seems to be kept entirely out of sight in Mr. Clark's report. He no where notices the all-important fact that the act of 1814 was passed upon the application of Trinity Church after full notice, and that the law was assented to by them. Here, then, were the two parties to the original compact—the Legislature representing the sovereign power of the State, and the corporation, whose rights were to be effected, concurring in an act modifying that compact. Although this view was most distinctly pre-sented in a pamphlet, to which Mr. Clark has referred at p. 18; yet, has he strangely overlooked it, and has discussed the whole question as if the act of 1814 had been passed, under the same circumstances as that of the Legislature of New-Hampshire in relation to Dartmouth College, against the will and consent of the corporation.

The corporation of Trinity Church represented to the Legislature that in the progress of events, a new state of things had arisen for which the existing compact between the government and the corporation had not provided, or that the provision, if any, was imperfect, and gave occasion to doubts and controversies. That state of things was, "that distinct corporations had been formed, each having its own peculiar endowments and places of worship, with rectors and other officers of their own choice, totally independent of any control or interference of your petitioners;" and further, "that individuals belonging to such separate congregations, have pretended to claim" the right of voting in the elections and regulating the affairs of Trinity Church. They therefore pray for an act "to alter the name of this corporation, and also to obviate and settle *the questions that might arise in consequence of incorporating other Episcopal congregations in the city of New-York.*" Let it be observed that the petition asked for no law that could affect any other Episcopalians than those who belonged to such separate corporations, and the question and the only question upon that point, on which legislative interposition was asked, related to the individuals *belonging* to the other corporations. And such as will be shown presently, was the only effect of the law of 1814, and that it left other Episcopalians precisely where they were before the passage of the act.

Now, with what propriety can it be said that an act passed for such a purpose, to obviate and settle questions arising out of an imperfect previous act of the Legislature, was not legislative and was judicial? It was an amendment of a legislative act in particulars, which subsequent circumstances had rendered ineffectual. It is the province of all sound legislation to protect citizens in the free and undisturbed enjoyment of their rights whether natural or acquired. There was an evil threatening the peace and prosperity of a respectable body of citizens having corporate rights. That body, by its legitimate representatives, proposed a modification of the compact to the other contracting party, which was assented to and adopted. Is this the manner in which courts of justice proceed?

The very act of 1784, which it was asked to amend, had been passed in the same way. Can it be said that that act was judicial?

An act to remove doubts respecting the charter rights of the ministers, elders and deacons of the Reformed Dutch Church of the city of New-York was passed in the same year, which confirmed elections and appointments, notwithstanding their want of conformity to the charter, and which abrogated an important power of assessing upon the members of the church, the expenses of maintaining its ministers and officers, and repairing it, &c.

Numerous acts of a similar character are found in the laws of almost every session since the organization of the government. Charters of every description, charitable, religious, banking, insurance, library, manufacturing—have been, from time to time, amended to explain or correct ambiguities or errors; to enlarge, to modify, and to diminish the corporate powers in matters affecting the interests of stockholders; upon the application of the trustees, directors or other official representatives of such corporations. They more or less give construction to previous acts, and generally supply their deficiencies. Was the power thus exercised judicial, or was it legislative? A distinguishing feature of a judicial act is, that it declares what the law has been and is, while a legislative act operates prospectively and declares what the law shall be. The judicial act affects cases of the like nature which have already occurred and declares the law by which they are to be governed.

Of the same general character are the statutes to be found in our session laws so profusely, confirming official acts of justices and other officers, irregularly elected, or qualified, and acts confirming titles of heirs and widows or of purchasers from them.

In the cases of corporations, the contract is made between the government and the body corporate, in its corporate charter, and not with its individual members. They are not known individually; they are merged in the body politic, and are represented by its officers, and necessarily bound by their acts. The very principle of their organization is, that the majority control and regulate the body; and the officers chosen by the majority, are its agents.

In *the Bank of Augusta* vs. *Earle*, 13 Peters 587, Ch. J. Taney giving the opinion of the court, says, "Whenever a corporation makes a contract it is the contract of the legal entity; of the artificial being created by the charter; and not the contract of the individual members."

Mr. Willcock in his treatise on corporations, p. 202, says, "The cases which have been determined on the presumption that the right of election may be restricted by a new charter, are so numerous that the question seems to be no longer controvertible."

In the case of *The Lincoln and Ken. Bank* vs. *Richardson*, 1 Greenleaf's Rep. 79, it was held by the Supreme Court of Maine, that the stockholders of a bank are bound by every act which amounts to an acceptance of the terms of the charter, on the part of the directors.

Upon no other principle than this, that those representing a corporation by virtue of their election, may assent to modifications of the charter, in good faith, can any one justify the numerous laws to be found extending acts of incorporation, enlarging or diminishing the capitals originally authorized, and in a variety of ways affecting the interests of individual stockholders. To deny the principle, would be to sweep from the statute books a large portion of the laws they contain.

As acts of incorporation of private eleemosynary institutions, are admitted on all hands to be contracts between the government and the corporation, they are subject to the provisions of the constitution of the United States, which forbids any State from impairing the obligation of contracts. The effect of this, is to create an entire dissimilarity between charters granted by the British parliament and those given by our State Legislatures, in respect to the power of repeal or modification. While the parliament by its constitution has such power, the King does not possess it, without the assent of the corporation. Says Justice Story in Dartmouth College *vs.* Woodward, 4 Wheaton, p. 676; "When a private eleemosynary corporation is thus created by the *charter of the crown* it is subject to no other control on the part of the crown, than what is expressly or implicitly reserved by the charter itself. Unless a power be reserved for this purpose, the crown can not by virtue of its prerogative, *without the consent of the corporation,* alter or amend the charter, or divest the corporation of any of its franchises, or add to them, or add or diminish the number of the trustees, or remove any of the members, or change or control the administration of the charity, or compel the corporation to receive a new charter. This is the uniform language of the authorities, and forms one of the most stubborn and well settled doctrines of the common law."

It is submitted that this is a full and accurate description of the limitations of the power of our State Legislatures under the constitution of the United States, and that whatever may be predicated of the power of the crown in reference to the corporations created by it, may be of the State Legislatures. Now, in the case of *the King* vs. *Miller,* in 6th Term Rep. 276, Lord Kenyon, giving the opinion of the King's bench says, "Where a corporation takes its rise from the King's charter, the King by granting and the corporation by accepting another charter, may alter it, because it is done with the consent of all the parties who are competent to consent to the alteration." This consent may be given by the corporators, or a majority of them, expressly by some formal act; or it may be presumed and inferred from repeated acts under the alterations, evincing their acquiesence and sanction. In the case of *The Bank of the U. S.* vs. *Danbridge,* 12 Wheaton, 70, 71, the judge delivering the opinion of the Supreme Court of the U. S., says: "In short we think the acts of artificial persons afford the same presumptions, as the acts of natural persons. Each affords presumptions from acts done, of what must have preceded them, as matters of right, or matters of duty." "So in relation to the question of the *acceptance of a particular charter* by an *existing corporation,* or by corporators already in the exercise of corporate functions, the acts of the corporate officers are admissible evidence from which the fact of acceptance may be inferred. It is not indipensable to show a written instrument or vote of acceptance on the corporation books. It may be inferred from other facts, which demonstrate that it must have been accepted." In the present case, the acts not only of the corporate officers, but of the corporators, in acquiescing in the provisions of this act of 1814, and in a uniform course of electing wardens and vestrymen according to those provisions, for more than thirty years, afford the most satisfactory and conclusive evidence of the acceptance of that act.

In most cases it must be impracticable to obtain the previous concurrence of all the corporators, to any modification of a charter, and the consequence of requiring it, would be to prevent the most salutary amendments, beneficial to the corporators themselves. To avoid such consequences, the constant practice has been to amend and modify charters upon the application of the officers of the corporation, in the first instance ; and these alterations are deemed to have been assented to by the whole body of corporators, unless objections by a majority of them, are made at the time, or within a reasonable period afterwards.

The Legislature has repeatedly acted upon this principle, in requiring the assent of the corporation under its corporate seal, to alterations in its charter, instead of requiring any expression from the individual corporators ; thus recognizing the authority of the corporation by its officers, to give a valid and binding consent. Thus in 1829, after the passage of the act to create the safety fund, some thirty bank charters were renewed, and in all the acts of renewal the following clause is found : " The charter of the said corporation shall not be extended by virtue of this act unless the said corporation shall, on or before the fourth day of January next, cause to be filed with the comptroller of this State, a certificate under its corporate seal and signed by its president and cashier, setting forth that the said corporation assents to become subject to all the provisions of this act." Session Laws of 1829, p. 465.

The act of 1837, suspending certain provisions of law respecting banks, and containing important restrictions upon their powers, has a similar provision in sec. 8, that it should not take effect in relation to certain banks until they should signify their assent to its provisions, by an agreement under their corporate seals, to be filed with the Secretary of State.

Indeed, so far as the legislation of this State bears upon the question, there has been one uniform invariable course, of which numerous instances might be cited like those already given, and there is not a solitary case to be found, where the assent of individual corporators to an alteration of the charter, has been required. Surely such a legislative construction, not questioned by any and acquiesced in by all, is entitled to great respect and consideration.

In this country the power of a corporation to dissolve itself by the act of a majority, seems admitted by all judges who have spoken on the point; see the cases collected in Angel and Ames on corporations, p. 507. But in this State the question has been put to rest by a legislative act. The 3d article of title 4, chap. 8, part 3 of the Rev. Stat., (vol. 2, p. [382,] 468,) provides, that whenever the directors, trustees, or other officers who have the management of the concerns of any corporation, or a majority of them, shall for any reason deem it beneficial to the interests of the stockholders, that such corporation should be dissolved, they may apply to the Chancellor for that purpose, who is authorized on such application to dissolve it accordingly. This law was originally passed in 1817. It is not prospective, but in terms includes existing corporations. Thus the principle is most distinctly recognized that the directors and trustees of corporations may affect the rights and interests of stockholders by giving up their charter without their assent to the particular act, or without any other assent than what is implied from the nature of corporate organizations and from the election of directors. It is true the Legislature did not think proper to extend this particular law to library societies, to religious corporations, or to select schools or academies. But the act proceeds upon the assumption that the power exists in all corporations, and regulates its exercise. If it did not exist, the act could not confer it, especially in reference to corporations then in being. Indeed this power of dissolution by surrender seems admitted in all the cases which have occurred in this State. *Slee* vs. *Broom*, 19 *John.*, 456. *Briggs* vs. *Penniman*, 1 *Hopkins*, 300 ; 8 *Cowen*, 387.

An extraordinary remark occurs at p. 26 of Mr. Clark's report, which certainly must have been made without due reflection. It is, that the act of 1814 was passed " without any investigation of the facts, any examinations of the law, or any hearing of the parties." Now it appears from the extracts from the proceedings of the two houses, appended to the memorial, and to which Mr. Clark has referred in another part of his report, that a remonstrance against the bill was presented to the Senate on the 18th of March; that it was discussed in committee of the whole both in the Senate and Assembly; that it was referred to the Attorney-General for his opinion on the law of the case ; that it was again debated in the Assembly, when a motion to reject it was negatived by a vote of 66 to 23. It would be difficult to furnish stronger evidence respecting any statute which has ever passed the Legislature, that the parties were heard, that the facts were investigated, (indeed, there was not a single fact in dispute,) and that the law had been fully and thoroughly examined.

III. The third reason given by Mr. Clark, as stated at p. 12, for recommending a repeal of the act of 1814, and as expanded at p. 29, 30, &c., is, that the terms of that act dispense with certain qualifications of the corporators, that were deemed essential to the character and purity of Trinity Church, and may change the location and character of the corporators.

The members of Trinity Church and other episcopalians, will probably be astonished to learn from Mr. Clark's report that the act of 1814 "abandoned *all* the *securities*" for preserving the religious character of Trinity Church.* One of these securities is said in the report of Mr. Clark, to have been found in the *name* given to the corporation by the act of 1788, of "the rector and inhabitants, &c., in communion of the protestant episcopal church in the State of New-York." A name would be but a slight and feeble security against a church abandoning episcopal doctrine and worship, when its members had renounced them. If there be such virtue in a name, the colonial act of 1704 must come under condemnation. For the charter of 1697 had called the corporation "the rector and inhabitants, &c., in communion of our protestant church of England, as now established by our laws;" but the colonial act suppressed the word "protestant," that all-important and emphatic word which has found such favor in Mr. Clark's report, and entirely omitted it in designating the corporation.

Another "security" for the character and purity of Trinity Church, Mr. C. thinks is found in the 3d section of the act of 1784, which describes the persons who shall be deemed corporators, as those "professing themselves members of the Episcopal church." This security, Mr. C. says (p. 29) is *forfeited* by its not being required in the act of 1814. Mr. Clark would not venture on the positive assertion that this qualification is *repealed* by the act of 1814, but his whole argument on this point is founded on that assumption. There is nothing in the act of 1814 at all inconsistent with the qualification in the act of 1784, requiring the corporators to profess themselves members of the Episcopal church. The well settled rules of construction (which will be more fully noticed here-

---

* On this subject as well as in reference to the *charge* against the committee of the vestry, who procured the passage of the act of 1814, that they either through ignorance or mistake, omitted to inform the Legislature that the act of 1704 was yet. (as Mr. Clark supposes,) a valid, existing law, it may be proper to copy from the printed remonstrance the names of the gentlemen who were members of it, viz: Richard Harison, David M. Clarkson, Thomas Barrow, Robert Troup, Jacob Le Roy, Peter Aug. Jay and Thos. Ludlow Ogden. Not a few of the memorialists themselves must be surprised to learn that however recreant to their duty the others might have been, Mr. JAY could have consented to accept a law that abandoned all the securities of Protestantism.

after) require that all statutes on the same subject shall be considered together, and full effect be given to each; and the application of them to
this case would require that a person offering himself to vote under the
act of 1814, should possess all the qualifications required by all the acts
on the subject, except those which had been repealed.

The position heretofore advanced, is also maintained, that the phrase
"forming part of the same religious corporation" contained in the act of
1814, in itself prescribes the condition that the persons offering to vote
shall be corporators according to the laws then in force. It is insisted
with entire confidence, that the expression "forming part of the same
religious corporation" applies to the first antecedent in the same 2d
section—"all male persons," and not to "the chapels belonging to
the same"—on account of the manifest absurdity of saying that a
chapel forms a part of *a corporation.* But it is unnecessary to spend time
in the discussion of that question, because the position already established
is sufficient—that the provision in question in the act of 1784 is not repealed
by the act of 1814. It is to be hoped that this view will relieve Mr. Clark,
and all others from their painful apprehensions arising from their supposition that Trinity Church is released from the obligation of being a protestant church. Upon the principle already stated, of considering all the
charters and laws bearing upon the subject, and giving them full operation, from the charter of 1697 to the act of 1814, Trinity Church must
not only remain a protestant church, but must continue an *episcopal*
church, in communion with the protestant episcopal church in the State
of New-York and in the United States; neither the corporation nor its
members can renounce the authority of bishops or the canons or rubrics of
the church—nor can they dispense with or mutilate the prayers and
order of religious worship set forth in the book of Common Prayer. All
the securities which ever existed to protect the corporation and its members from popery on the one hand and from the doctrines and forms of
worship of other religious denominations on the other, are still maintained in their original vigor and strength.

It is hoped that it may be permitted, without disrespect to the senato-
rial character, to express deep regret that an official public document like
the report of a member of a committee of one branch of the Legislature,
should contain statements and intimations in relation to the differences on
theological questions, known to exist in the episcopal church, exceedingly
offensive to a portion of that denomination, and which as they have no
bearing whatever on the legal or constitutional questions involved, are introduced without any necessity or excuse. Had the report been prepared
by one of the heated zealots who have made themselves conspicuous for

their intolerance and arrogance—who assume the very infallibility which they deprecate, and seek to proscribe their brethren for an adherence to what they conscientiously believe to be the true and sound doctrines of their church in the days of its greatest purity—had the report been prepared by one, who in a whole life of religious controversy had evinced any thing but charity, it could not have contained more unjust, or more intolerant reflections. Our Constitution has wisely prohibited all discriminations on account of religious belief, and hitherto our Legislative assemblies have adhered to the spirit of this provision, and have scrupulously avoided all discussions of such topics as calculated only to excite intolerance, disorder and contention.

It is believed that there are very few instances in which legislative reports have been of a different character, previous to that under consideration. The same Senator did indeed indulge himself in allusions of a similar description in a report presented by him to the Senate in 1845, in relation to changing the name of a public school society.

Trinity Church has no concern with these contentions, and as her rights are in no way connected with them, they should not be made dependent on them. The corporation has taken and will take no part in them. Individual members will espouse such views as their consciences dictate, and whether they be right or wrong, the corporate authorities have neither right nor pretension to enquire. It is insisted that such discussions are improperly mingled with the matters before the Legislature. They divert attention from the true merits of the controversy, and substitute feeling and prejudice for judgment and discretion. Their introduction is therefore deprecated as improper in itself and unjust to the corporation— and to those who are assailed. The latter are entitled under our blessed constitution to "the free exercise and enjoyment of their religious profession and worship without discrimination," and without molestation from any source, whether they belong to either extreme of the opposing parties, or are between the two. When Trinity Church or any other corporation diverts the funds entrusted to its care, to uses and purposes variant from the intentions of the donors or the policy of the State, the judicial tribunals will be found armed with abundant powers to deprive the offending corporation of all control over those funds, and to declare its dissolution for any abuse of its franchises. It cannot be pretended that the repeal or the continuance of the act of 1814, would either prevent such abuse, or add to, or diminish, the powers of the courts to correct it. How then could the apprehension, real or affected, of such abuse, influence the action of the Legislature upon the memorials presented to it? Those memorials presented no such ground for legislative interposition.

And it may be supposed without questioning the astuteness of Mr. Clark, that those who prepared the memorials and the accompanying argument, were at least as well acquainted with the appropriate grounds on which their application was to be sustained, as he could be. They had no such apprehensions, or if they had, they considered them unfit to be presented to the consideration of a legislative body.

There is another omission in the act of 1814, which Mr. Clark's report presents as a reason for its repeal, and which he considers not quite so *alarming* in its possible consequences as that last mentioned, and this is stated at p. 31, to be the omission to re-enact in the description of the corporators, that they must be inhabitants of the city of New-York. The report says that this limitation is retained in the acts of 1784 and 1788, but is not found in the act of 1814. The answer already given covers this objection. All the statutes in relation to Trinity Church are to be considered and construed together, being in *pari materia*, and no provision in one is repealed, unless by express words, or by necessary implication in consequence of its repugnancy to a subsequent provision.* It might with equal propriety be said that the wardens and vestrymen had no authority to choose a rector, because no such provision is found in the act of 1814, or that no election could be had, because neither the number of wardens and vestrymen to be chosen, nor the time of the election, were provided, either in the act of 1784 or in that of 1814. These acts were supplements to those previously existing, and provided for the special cases for which they were intended.

---

* These principles seem so entirely to have escaped Mr. Clark's recollection; and the whole of his third reason for the repeal of the act of 1814, being founded on the misapprehension that the provisions of the charter of 1697 and of the act of 1784, are not to be regarded in determining the qualifications of voters uuder the act of 1814, that it seems advisable to quote a few leading authorities on the subject. In his 20th lecture, Chancellor Kent says: "Several acts in *pari materia* and relating to the same subject, are to be taken together, and compared in the construction of them, because they are considered as having one object in view, and as acting upon one system; and the rule applies, though some of the statutes may have expired *or are not referred to* in the other acts."

In *McCartee* vs. *Orphan Asylum*, 9 Cowen, 437, it was held by the court for the Correction of Errors, that " Two statutes shall stand together and both have effect, if possible; for the law does not favor repeals by implication; and all acts in *pari materia* should be taken together, as if they were one law." 1 Black. Comm. 89, 90. " And an old statute gives place to a new one. But this is to be understood only when the latter statute is couched in negative terms, or where its matter is so clearly repugnant that it necessarily implies a negative." " But if both acts be merely affirmative, and the substance such that both may stand together, here the latter does not repeal the former, but they shall have a concurrent efficacy."

The act of 1814 was passed to obviate and settle doubts in relation to a particular qualification of persons who claimed to be corporators and electors, and it left all other qualifications as it found them, with the exception of dispensing with the requisite of having paid for the support of the church.

There is not a word to be found in it inconsistent with the qualifications that the voters should be inhabitants of the city of New-York, and that they should profess themselves members of the Protestant Episcopal Church. If these were qualifications before the act, they remain so still. The fundamental error of the report has been, that it considered the 2d section of the act of 1814 a repeal of all former provisions on the same subject; whereas, it is not negative but affirmative in its character, and specifies certain qualifications, which those claiming to vote, should possess. It dispenses with none that were previously required, except the single one before mentioned, of paying to the support of the church. It is submitted then, that Mr. Clark's third reason for the repeal wholly fails, because the fact on which it is founded does not exist.

The affirmative provision which it contains requiring voters to be members of the congregation of Trinity church or of one of its chapels, may be defended and justified upon general grounds without reference to any previous charter or law. The meaning of the phrase is sufficiently given in Mr. Clark's report, p. 17, which says, "it denotes all persons who usually assemble for public worship in the same church." Can it be supposed that any church of any denomination could be maintained, in which the trustees, vestrymen, rector, and other officers were to be chosen or appointed by any others than those who "usually assemble in it for public worship," and who form the body for whose use the society and all its incidents were created? Are clergymen in our churches to be called by persons who are not to hear them, and who are to take no part in the services of the sanctuary where they are to officiate? Are strangers, though belonging to the same general denomination, to select preachers for congregations to which they do not belong? Is it not necessarily implied from the very nature of any society or association, that those only are to control its affairs who belong to it? And shall a congregation of a christian church be the only exception? It is affirmed with entire confidence, that in the absence of any provision on the subject in any act of incorporation, common sense and common justice would prescribe as the very first and elementary qualification to a person's exercising any control in the affairs of any congregation, that he should belong to it, and be a member of it. And the act of 1814 therefore, very properly inserted a declaration to that effect, that the members of other congregations might not presume to interfere with one to which they did not belong. And this was the sole and whole effect of this provision. It is not correct, as intimated at p. 27 of Mr. Clark's report, that " all that class of Episcopalians in the city of New-York who are not members of any congregation as such in the city," are excluded from voting by the act of 1814. They have the same right to qualify themselves to be voters which they had before that act; and if they are excluded from voting, it is because they do not choose to avail themselves ·of the right. It might with equal truth be affirmed that they were excluded by the act of 1784, which required them to hold pews or be communicants. Any qualification whatever that should be prescribed, would exclude them until they complied with it. They are excluded by the act of 1814 precisely as presbyterians, methodists, and members of other denominations are, and in no other way, namely: so long as they refuse to participate in the privileges offered them, by refusing to become members of the congregation. It is the result of their own choice—the law does not exclude them. If they are episcopalians, they have but to become members of the congregation of Trinity Church, "to worship usually" in that church or in one of its chapels, and they at once become corporators and voters upon complying with the other conditions prescribed by the several acts. But from episcopalians who do not belong to any corporation, no complaint is heard. The memorials to the Legislature, proceed wholly from those who belong to *other* incorporated episcopal churches, and are members of the congregations of those churches. These, and these only, ask that all the guaranties which secure to the members of the corporation of Trinity church, the government and control of their own affairs, should be swept away, and its elections thrown open to an indiscriminate multitude, belonging to other churches, or belonging to none, upon no other qualification than that they are inhabitants of New-York, and profess to belong to the Episcopal church. This is in truth the result which all their representations and arguments are calculated to produce.

It is time to hasten to a conclusion. Mr. Clark's report urges the repeal of the whole act óf 1814 instead of the particular sections complained of by the memorialists. The third section, confirming grants made by the church, the report considers useless if such grants were originally valid; and if they were not valid, that then the Legislature had no right to confirm them. The best answer to this remark is furnished by the second section of the bill which Mr. Clark has reported, which forbids the corporation from disputing the validity of any of its grants *before* or since the passage of the act of 1814, by which it would have been bound under that act;

which is but a circumlocutive manner of declaring that the grants shall be valid; thus re-enacting the identical provision he proposes to repeal. A stronger admission of the propriety of the third section of the act of 1814 could not be made. The fourth section of the act of 1814, stands upon the same ground, being only more particular in referring specially to the grants to St. George's Church. It would also be saved by the second section of Mr. Clark's bill. Would it not have been more simple and direct not to repeal those sections at all, than thus to repeal and then re-enact them?

The 5th section of the act of 1814 authorizes an amicable separation of the congregation of any chapel of Trinity Church, by the consent of the congregation and the corporation, and provides that when such agreement is made the members of such congregation shall cease to be members of the corporation of Trinity Church, and may incorporate themselves. This section also, Mr. Clark proposes to repeal. He would not even permit persons voluntarily to renounce their connexion with Trinity Church. He would bind them perpetually to that corporation. He says, "each of these sections, (the 3d, 4th and 5th,) involves a plain exercise of judicial power, or such an alteration of the chartered rights of Trinity Church, as it was not within the competence of the Legislature to establish." It is not deemed necessary to waste a word on this idea of a prospective judicial power in authorizing parties to make future arrangements respecting the partition of their common property. And as to chartered rights, it has hitherto been supposed that when an act is authorized to be done, upon the consent of all persons interested, there could be no question raised respecting the violation of the rights of those parties. At p. 35 the report regards these sections as quite useless, and says, that the validity of the separations by mutual consent would not be affected by a repeal of them. But that is a small part of the question. Future separations will be as necessary hereafter as they have been heretofore; and the law which allows them in a peaceable, orderly and regular manner, and defines with precision the consequences, is in itself valuable, and can not be repealed without mischievous results.

The 6th section of the act of 1814 is a general provision applicable to religious corporations in the cities of New-York, Albany and Schenectady, and intended to exempt them from a very unnecessary and vexatious burthen. By the 10th section of the general act for religious corporations (3d Rev. Stat. p. 210) the treasurer or trustees of churches in New-York, Albany or Schenectady, (and it is not required of churches in any other place,) are required once in every three years to exhibit an account of their estate to the chancellor or a judge of the supreme court or of the county courts, and in case of omission to do so, the corporation is dissolved. Now, the 6th section of the act of 1814 provides that this account need not be rendered unless the church has acquired other lands subsequent to the rendering of an account. Mr. Clark has entirely mis-conceived the original act when he speaks of the religious societies hav-ing been required by it to make an annual report to the Legislature. There was no such provision. The judge to whom the account was de-livered, if he found the amount of the estate owned by a church greater than that allowed by law, was to report the inventory to the Legislature. It is evident that the provision of the act of 1814 is just as effectual to secure a knowledge of the fact that any church in the above mentioned cities has exceeded its income, as the original law; and there can be no reason whatever for restoring that law. Still, if it is deemed necessary or proper to do so, it can easily be done by a separate act.

An unwillingness is felt to close these remarks without adverting to a singular omission in the report of Mr. Clark, to pay the least attention to the argument which was pressed before the committee by those who represented Trinity Church, and which has been reiterated on various oc-casions and in various forms, that the long acquiescence for more than thirty years in the provisions of the act of 1814 by those immediately and directly affected, is in itself a sufficient reason why the Legislature should not now interpose, and by an act of at least doubtful authority, throw open the flood-gates of contention and litigation. Why Mr. Clark has not thought proper to discuss this point, does not appear.

A brief recapitulation of the points presented in these remarks will be convenient and perhaps useful.

I. Mr. Clark repudiates and rejects the grounds presented by the memo-rialists for the repeal of the act of 1814, as wholly insufficient, because a repeal on those grounds would be a judicial act.

II. He nevertheless argues that the act was unconstitutional and should be repealed in order to remove an impediment to the legal assertion of the rights of the complainants; and in effect calls upon the Legisla-ture to act judicially in determining whether those rights have been in-vaded.

III. He pays no attention to the fact that the act of 1814 was passed with the assent and on the application of the corporation through their legitimate representatives; and does not discriminate between the power of the Legislature to modify a compact with the consent of the other party, as was done in 1814, and its power to change and alter the compact thus modified, without the consent and against the remonstrance of the other contracting party.

5

IV. He omits all notice of the admitted fact, that all parties interested in the matter have acquiesced in the act of 1814 for more than thirty years.

V. He assumes grounds for recommending the repeal of that act which never occurred to the memorialists, and which are wholly unfounded in fact.

VI. The first reason assigned by him for the repeal, that the act of 1814 was procured by the suppression of a statute printed among the public laws, and by misrepresenting of that statute as being repealed, is inconsistent in itself, is contradicted by the facts, and could not be true.

VII. If any representations were made, and if the act of 1814 was passed on the belief, that the colonial act of 1704 was repealed by the act of 1784, they were perfectly true and accurate in all respects.

VIII. The second reason assigned by Mr. Clark for the repeal, that the act of 1814 was a judicial construction and determination of the rights of the corporators, is unsound. It was strictly legislative, partaking in no respect of the character of a judicial decision; and it was en-entirely within the competence of the Legislature, in order to correct imperfections and defects in former laws, which rendered them inapplicable to a new state of things that had arisen. Such acts, passed with the consent of the trustees or other officers representing the corporation, and acquiesced in by the body of the corporators, are coeval with our government, and a denial of the principle at this day would overturn hundreds of statutes, affect vitally most important rights and interests, and produce endless and intolerable confusion.

IX. The third reason given by Mr. Clark for the repeal is, that the act of 1814 "*dispenses with*" qualifications of corporators, essential to the preservation of the character and purity of Trinity Church, and may change the location and character of the corporators;—and that the change in the name of the corporation also exposes it to lose its distinctive religious character.

1. It is denied that a change of name can have any such effect, when the peculiar character of the corporation is indicated by the provisions of its charter; and it is also denied that a single qualification of corporators that existed before the act of 1814 is "dispensed with" by that act, except the single one of paying to the support of the church ; but

2. On the contrary it is maintained upon the the clearest and best settled principles of law, that all the acts and charters in relation to Trinity Church form one body of laws upon the same subject, which are to have full effect and operation in every particular in which they have not been

repealed in express terms or by a subsequent repugnant provision. And as there has been no such repeal of the qualifications referred to, of being inhabitants of New-York and professing to be members of the episcopal church, they are still required ; and all the securities and guaranties of the religious character of Trinity Church and of the proper employment of its funds, are retained in full vigor. That the remedy for any perversion of its funds, is to be found in the courts of justice, and not in the repeal of an act which in no way affects the guards or remedies against such perversion.

Lightning Source UK Ltd.
Milton Keynes UK
UKHW010910220119
335966UK00008B/520/P